CONTENTS

HOW TO USE THIS BOOK

The exciting, interactive adventure stories in this book feature puzzles on every page. When you reach a puzzle, stop! You must "unlock" the next part of story by solving that problem. Don't skip ahead until you've worked out the answer! Check that your solution is correct by turning to the back of the book.

It's worth having some scrap paper handy for any working out. Give each puzzle your best shot, and don't worry if you get some answers wrong first time—you can still carry on with the story and try again later.

HAPPY ADVENTURING!

MATHS ADVENTURES

Solve the puzzles, save the world!

ARCTURUS

ARCTURUS

This edition published in 2019 by Arcturus Publishing Limited
26/27 Bickels Yard, 151–153 Bermondsey Street,
London SE1 3HA

Author: William Potter
Illustrator: Rayanne Vieira
Editor: Sebastian Rydberg and Joe Harris
Designer: Amy McSimpson

ISBN: 978-1-78828-636-7
CH006240NT
Supplier 29, Date 0319, Print run 7078

Printed in China

STEM+
SCIENCE TECHNOLOGY ENGINEERING MATHEMATICS

What is STEM?

STEM is a world-wide initiative
that aims to cultivate an
interest in Science, Technology,
Engineering, and Mathematics,
in an effort to promote these
disciplines to as wide a variety of
students as possible.

THE INFINITY SQUAD
IN HEROES VS. ZERO!

THE INFINITY SQUAD

Meet Prime City's number-one heroes, champions of freedom, and masters of mathematics.

DOC ZERO

Our mysterious villain. Who is behind the mask, and what is the rogue's bizarre plan?

OPTIMAN

His bravery, strength, and resilience are greater than most people's, as is his vanity!

MR. CALCULUS

Super-intelligent team leader and computer genius. He can mathematically prove that geeks rule.

MULTI-GIRL

This quick-thinking hero can create copies of herself to confuse enemies and help in emergencies.

Hooray for the heroes! In Prime City's main square, Mayor Zilch prepares to unveil a magnificent statue of the Infinity Squad, created by internationally famous sculptor Paco de Nada.

A large crowd has gathered to see both the artist and the city's greatest champions. *Daily Comet* reporter Natalie Nil is there to report on the Mayor's speech.

Thank you all for coming today to celebrate Prime City's own super-team. The Infinity Squad has saved the city too many times to remember...

Can you work out exactly how many times Prime City has been saved by the Infinity Squad? Look at Mr. Calculus' graph for the last five years to work it out.

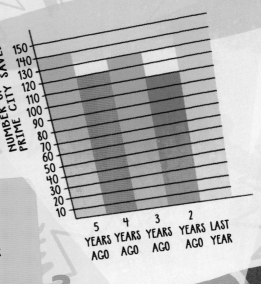

As the curtain is drawn back, the crowd gasps.
The statues have been covered in graffiti! Who could
have done this to the city's popular defenders?
"I can think of exactly 166 individuals," says Mr. Calculus.
Detective Noughtie, who has just arrived on the scene,
scratches his head.

The statues have been covered with numbers!

The numbers painted on the statues are all exactly
divisible by three—except for one. Which number is it?

Multi-Girl takes a closer look and
discovers a secret compartment under
the odd number out. Inside is
a combination lock.

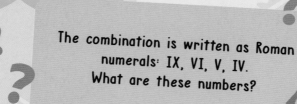

The combination is written as Roman
numerals: IX, VI, V, IV.
What are these numbers?

When Multi-Girl enters the combination, the numbers change
to 1,000, and start counting down with a loud ticking.
"My statue has a bomb inside it!" Optiman gasps.
"Evacuate the square!" orders the Mayor.
Mr. Calculus remains calm, and studies
the countdown carefully...

Optiman, get ready to
hurl the statue into the
air at the last second!

The countdown from 1,000
is going down by 25 every
second. How many seconds
until it reaches zero?

Just in time, Optiman hurls his
statue into the air, where
it explodes harmlessly, and
turns into a shower of dust.

The mid-air explosion causes an invisible ship to appear.

Looks like the villain has been revealed!

Aboard the mysterious O-ship, the nefarious Doc Zero hammers on the ship's failing invisibility controls in a temper tantrum.

Curse the Infinity Squad for their blind luck. That dust has broken my ship's clever cloaking device!

1 4 9 – 25 36 –
1 1 2 3 5 8 – 21
81 72 – 54 – 36 27

To repair the cloaking device, Doc Zero must retype the missing numbers in the three sequences on the screen. Can you work out what they are? Each row has a different sequence.

The Infinity Squad leaps into action. Optiman jumps from block to block of the disappearing tower to reach the O-ship, but Doc Zero uses the Null-Ray to blast all the even-numbered blocks from under his feet.

Find a path for Optiman, stepping only on adjoining odd-numbered blocks.

Multi-Girl tries to confuse Doc Zero by duplicating herself to provide extra targets.

Can't hit one Multi-Girl? How about five?

If she adds one duplicate every 15 seconds, and they last for one minute each, how many duplicates will be left after 10 minutes?

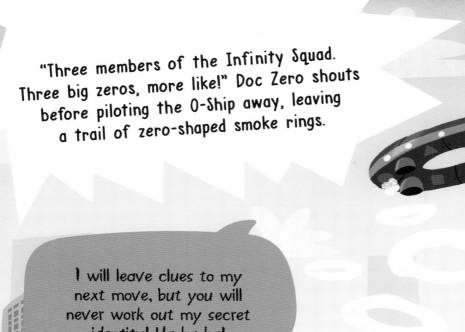

"Three members of the Infinity Squad. Three big zeros, more like!" Doc Zero shouts before piloting the O-Ship away, leaving a trail of zero-shaped smoke rings.

I will leave clues to my next move, but you will never work out my secret identity! Ha ha ha!

I think I can catch Doc Zero!

Optiman races a mile in 90 seconds, while Doc Zero's ship flies at 60 m.p.h. Will Optiman be able to catch up?

Doc Zero gets away, so the Infinity Squad returns to headquarters to figure out who he or she is. The clue could be in the name.

MAYOR ZILCH **PACO DE NADA** **DETECTIVE NOUGHTIE** **NATALIE NIL**

Mayor Zilch, the sculptor Paco De Nada, Detective Noughtie, and *Daily Comet* reporter Natalie Nil all have names that mean zero.

There's an urgent call from Prime City Police. Doc Zero is using the Null-Ray again to destroy buildings. The team looks at the locations. There is a pattern. Read first by column, then by row: 1,4; 1,5; 1,7; 2,2; 2,3; 2,8; 2,9; 3,2; 3,9; 4,1; 4,10; 5,1; 6,1; 6,10; 7,1; 7,10; 8,2; 9,2; 9,3; 9,8; 9,9; 10,4; 10,6; 10,7.

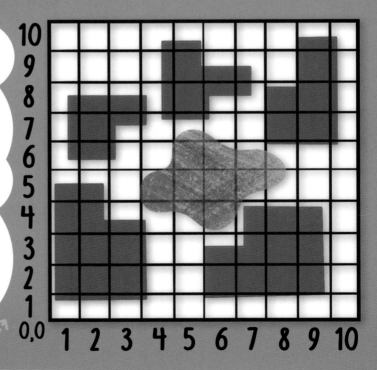

Mark the coordinates on the map of the city. They are forming a symmetrical pattern. What shape is it? There are four gaps—these are the next targets. What are their coordinates?

The Infinity Squad now knows the targets, but not the order. Where will Doc Zero strike next?

As if in answer to their question, the heroes get a call on their hotline. It's *Daily Comet* reporter Natalie Nil.

Hi, Optiman. Doc Zero has sent me clues. Can you help me decode them?

Hi, Natalie. What's up?

Doc Zero asked, "If the answer is always zero, what are the missing numbers? That's my next target."

$$24 \div 8 - ? = 0$$
$$2 \times 6 \div ? - 4 = 0$$
$$3 \times ? \div 3 - 7 = 0$$

The missing numbers are familiar—it's the address of the *Daily Comet*! The fiendish Doc Zero has been taunting the reporters with the news that they are the next target!

The Infinity Squad alerts the police to evacuate the building, and then decides on the quickest way to get there.

They have several options of how to get there.
The Infini-car has to go 6 miles at 120 m.p.h.
The Infini-cycle has to go 3 miles at 90 m.p.h.
The Infini-copter has to go 4 miles at 240 m.p.h.
A public bus has to go 2 miles at 60 m.p.h.
Which one would arrive first?

By the time the Squad reaches the *Daily Comet*, the building is empty, but Doc Zero has blasted through several windows on the top two floors of the building.

You're too late.

This time, yes, but Doc Zero has left us another clue to the next target!

And a big repair bill!

The clue is in the windows. Count the broken windows from top left to bottom right. There is a number sequence: 2, 3, 5, 7, 11, 13, and 17. What would the next two numbers in the sequence be?

Mr. Calculus deduces that Doc Zero's next target is on the corner of 19th and 23rd Street, and leads the team there. Back aboard the Infini-copter, Optiman compares a row of buildings to a poster of the scene before the attacks.

Look at the buildings before the attack. What fraction of each has disappeared?

Sure enough, they soon find Doc Zero's O-ship. Multi-Girl creates a duplicate of herself to land the Infini-copter, while the team leaps onto a nearby building to take on Doc Zero.

"Watch out!" Mr. Calculus cries, as Doc Zero opens fire with lethal laser beams.

"The beams are coming from the blaster cannons in order," spots Multi-Girl. "If we work out the order, we can dodge them!"

The cannons are firing in the order: 1, 3, 5, 2, 4, 6, 5, 3, 1... Can you spot the pattern and figure out which cannons will fire the next three rays?

1   2   3   4   5   6

Aboard the O-ship, devious Doc Zero orders the computer to calculate an attack plan using mecha-missiles.

If I hit Optiman enough times, he will fall, for sure!

The computer produces four attack plans: A, B, C, and D. Each target shows missile strikes and how much each strike will score. Only a score of 50 is enough to knock out Optiman. Which attack plan should Doc Zero choose?

Doc Zero fires the mecha-missiles, but Optiman swats them away with a girder. However, the building he is standing on has been hit and is now about to collapse.

> We need to prop up the tower so the residents can escape!

> Optiman needs Multi-Girl to place blocks of equal strength next to the building. Which four blocks on the ground add up to the same number as the four on the building?

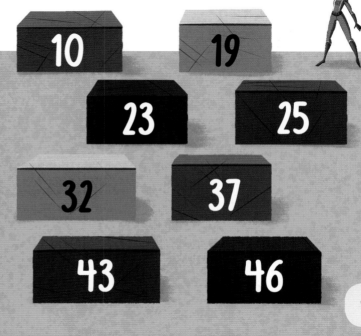

15

29

33

42

10   19

23   25

32   37

43   46

Multi-Girl creates copies of herself to help the residents and their pets escape from the building before it is destroyed.

Miaow!

Exactly! We don't want you to disappear with your home, do we?

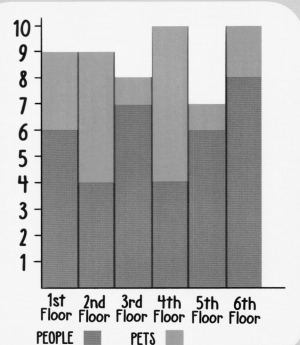

One Multi-Girl is needed to rescue every five residents, and one for every three pets. Look at the graph. How many Multi-Girls are needed in total?

PEOPLE   PETS

While nice people collect stickers or toys, villains like Doc Zero collect nasty weapons.

I have four Magno Mines, twice as many Stun Strikes as Magno Mines, plus three times as many Scare Flares as Stun Strikes... That should be more than enough to crush the Infinity Squad!

Doc Zero fires three Magno Mines, three times as many Scare Flares as Magno Mines, and four fewer Stun Strikes than Scare Flares. How many of each does he have left?

Mr. Calculus has found the ship's weakness! Now he hatches a plan to hack into Doc Zero's computer and turn off the weapons systems.

$$5 \times 3 \ ? \ 4 = 19$$
$$7 \ ? \ 2 + 11 = 25$$
$$9 \times 3 \ ? \ 6 = 21$$
$$30 \div 6 \ ? \ 12 = 17$$
$$4 \times 6 \ ? \ 3 = 8$$
$$33 \div 11 \ ? \ 12 = 15$$

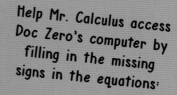

Help Mr. Calculus access Doc Zero's computer by filling in the missing signs in the equations:

+
−
÷
x

As planned, Doc Zero's computer weapons are shut down, but the guidance systems are also turned off. The O-ship goes out of control.

Optiman leaps from the Infini-copter to land on the O-ship.

I may be able to steer the ship by changing the balance of the ship's engine output.

Doc Zero's ship has four engines. They are all working at 100%. Optiman needs to reduce the power of the two front engines by 50% each, and the two rear engines by 30% each, to bring the ship down safely. If he does this, by what percentage will the O-ship's total engine output be reduced?

The loss of power is enough for Optiman to land the O-ship on Prime City's famous landmark, the Spire.

The Infinity Squad can now access the hatch below the ship, but they can't open it!

It's locked... but I can see an entry system!

Beside the hatch, there are six dials. They all have measures in degrees next to them, showing how much they need to turn clockwise to open the hatch. Mark the position each dial should be turned to.

0°　　90°　　45°　　180°　　270°　　135°

Multi-Girl opens the hatch, but Doc Zero is waiting for them, armed with a Null-Ray hand-blaster. Thinking quickly, Optiman rips the hatch door off its hinges, and uses it as a shield.

My Null-Ray will make your pathetic shield disappear in seconds... then it's your turn!

I don't like this villain's attitude.

The Null-Ray is causing the door to lose 5% of its original size every second. How long does the team have before it's completely gone?

Optiman has just enough time to use the door as a ram, and charges at Doc Zero. Unfortunately, the villain accidentally hits the ship's power supply with the Null-Ray.

Doc Zero panics as the power supply is damaged. A computer readout shows the power levels heading toward a dangerous overload. Mr. Calculus has to think quickly.

POWER SURPLUS

REDUCTOR A
19   23
14   17
12

$$41 - \square - \square = 0$$
$$38 - \square - \square = 0$$
$$34 - \square - \square = 0$$
$$27 - \square - \square = 0$$
$$25 - \square - \square = 0$$

REDUCTOR B
22   20
15   10
13

Keep hold of Doc Zero, Optiman! I need to make some hasty calculations to save the ship from blowing up!

Multi-Girl, duplicate yourself so you can check two monitors at once!

I don't care about you lot, but save me!

To stop the ship exploding, the Infinity Squad needs to drain the power surplus. Choose a number from the left screen and a number from the right screen and subtract these from a number on the central screen to make it equal zero.

It is a close thing, but the Infinity Squad manages to save the ship and capture Doc Zero. And look who he is... the famous sculptor Paco de Nada!

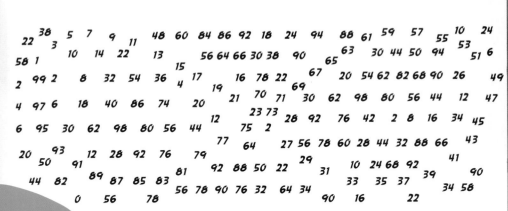

He is all yours, Detective!

I have reversed the effects of the Null-Ray. All the buildings are restored.

Making the city disappear would have been my greatest work of art!

You like art? They have lots of drawing books in prison!

The O-ship's computer has produced a series of numbers on its screen. Connect all the odd numbers together in increasing values. What shape is formed?

The Mystery of the Division Dragon

Meet Anna Kadabra and Cleo

When precious items go missing from the Mathmagical Museum, you need someone with special skills to find the culprit. Here is the best team for the job.

Anna Kadabra

Anna Kadabra is the country's leading wizard detective. Her special skills are mathmagic and number charms. She has used her working-out wand and the Arithmetic Amulet to successfully solve many calculated crimes.

Cleo

Cleo is a young sphinx who has been turned to stone to guard the magical relics of the Egyptian Pharaohs. She comes back to life to help Anna in her investigations.

3

6   80

17

0

5   22   41

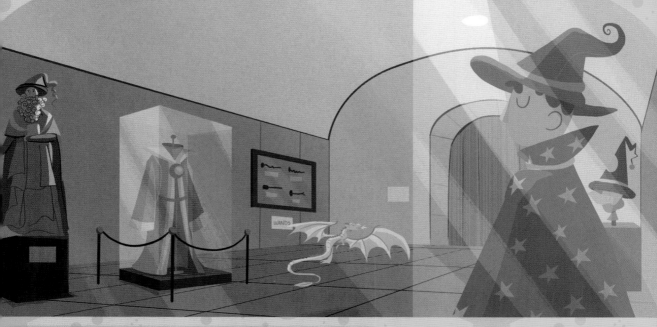

It's after hours at the Mathmagical Museum. The visitors are gone, and the lights are low. Everything is quiet, but something extraordinary is flying across the hall. A little green dragon uses its flaming breath to disable the Charm Alarm security system and enter Room 23.

3	4	5	6
×4	+10	×4	−4
+3	÷2	−2	×11
÷3	×3	÷6	+8
×6	−5	+20	÷5

6	30	16	23

The dragon has burned through the Charm Alarm wires. Can you repair them by reconnecting each vertical sequence to the correct number at the bottom? Start with the number at the top of a sequence, then carry out the calculations connected by the wires.

35

Room 23 is the Chamber of Ancient Egyptian Magic,
where Cleo the little sphinx stands guard.
The dragon slips in unnoticed, and casts
a spell to open the sarcophagus.

Can you wake Cleo from her ancient slumber, to stop
this sneaky dragon? Match six numbers in the room
with their squares to bring her back to life.
For example, $4^2 = 16$.

With the awakening spell unlocked, Cleo comes to life. She purrs as she opens her eyes, but then growls when she spots the dragon disappearing into the sarcophagus.

In the sarcophagus is the mummy of Thetsukah. On his head is a gold headdress covered with glittering gems, including the sacred pink scarab gem!

To remove the headdress, the dragon must press the one gem on the headdress without a line of symmetry. Which one is it?

With the headdress in his jaws, the dragon flies away in haste. Cleo gives chase, and the pair hurl simple magic spells to slow each other down.

Meoooowrrr!

The dragon stops, rips the pink ruby from the headdress with its claws, and drops it through a grille in the floor. Can Cleo stop the dragon escaping this way too?

The green dragon is launching decimals at Cleo. Help her fight back by matching the decimal numbers with her fractions.

The next morning, the museum's security guard has called in mathmagic detective Anna Kadabra to help. "Another stolen gem!" says Anna. "That's the eighth this month! Did you say a dragon escaped with the pink gem down this grille?"

"That's what the Charm Alarm security camera shows," says the guard. "That baby sphinx tried to squeeze in after the dragon, but she got stuck. That's where I found her this morning."

She talks in a strange language, and I cannot understand it.

Anna smiles and raises her wand. She has a translation spell that will help.

To make Anna's translation spell begin, work out what numbers the letters A, B, and C equal in this set of equations:

$$A + B = 10$$
$$C - A = 5$$
$$12 - B = 6$$

With the translation spell working, Anna talks to Cleo,
not in Ancient Egyptian, but in Ancient Cat!
"My name is Cleo, and I'm not a baby
sphinx!" Cleo insists. "I am
thousands of years old!"

"Nice to meet you, Cleo,"
says Anna. "I'm Anna,
the mathmagic detective.
Were you trying to
catch the thief?"

"That's my job," says Cleo. "I was turned to stone over 2,000 years ago,
to guard over Pharaoh Thetsukah's tomb, but not only have I been unable
to protect it, I've now lost his sacred scarab gem!" she sobs.
"Don't feel bad, Cleo," says Anna. "Together, I'm sure we can put things
right. Why do you think the dragon went after this specific object?"
"It's not the first magical gem to disappear," says the security guard.

The guard shows Anna and Cleo a picture of the other gems stolen. They
form a pattern. What would the next two gems be in the sequence?

Anna rubs her amulet. It shows her that the gems are in the museum, but not exactly where.

"They're not in the collection," says the guard.
"They must be in one of the museum's secret rooms."
"Secret rooms?" says Cleo. "How typical of a magic museum to have rooms that no one can find!"
"To find a secret room, we need a map!" cries Anna.
"I know where to find that," says Cleo with a smile,
"The map room! Look, there is the key."

To release the key, they need to complete the number tiles on the pyramid below. Adding two tiles together equals the number on the tile above them. Fill in the gaps to work out the numbers to the top.

Having worked out the missing numbers, the key magically appears in Anna's hand. Cleo takes her to the map room, and Anna opens the door. The room is full of ancient atlases and guide books to forgotten places. Curiously, there are several books with numbers on the spines. Suddenly, they hear a voice...

"Find the highest prime number."

It feels like we're following a trail! Which book has the highest prime number?

As Anna pulls the correct book from the shelf, a tiny, white dragon leaps from the top of the bookcase. It must have been his voice that they heard! Cleo yelps with surprise. The dragon tries to look as fierce as possible.

I am the custodian of the maps, and no one can read these magical tomes without first solving my riddle!

At first, I am 104. Halve me, halve me, and halve me again. What have I become?

When Anna answers correctly, the tiny dragon flaps back to the top of the bookcase and allows the pair to open the book. "Look, Cleo," says Anna, "There's a map tucked between the pages!" The map shows numbered hidden rooms in the Mathmagical Museum.

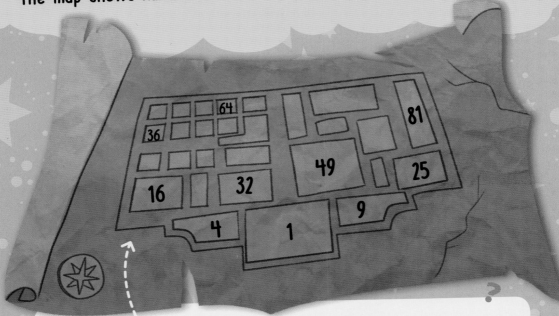

Only one of the rooms is not a square number. Which one?

Anna and Cleo decide they must go to that room. Before they leave, the white dragon says, "To find what you seek, you will need to look high, not low!" Then it disappears.
"I don't trust dragons," says Cleo, "but that one has been quite helpful." They head toward the secret room. Anna waves her wand at a wall where the door to the secret room should be. She casts a spell: "Unseen by mere mortal, reveal the magic portal!"
In a puff of magic, a doorway appears revealing a large stone circle.

As Anna is quick to realize, the standing stones are positioned as Roman numerals. Which stones represent the highest number?

The pair look closely at one of the stones. There are mysterious symbols carved into the surface. "It looks as if we need to match them up," says Anna. "But what happens if we do?" Cleo wonders aloud. She's starting to get nervous, but it's her job to get that gem back.

$\frac{1}{8}$

$\frac{1}{4}$

$\frac{1}{3}$

$\frac{1}{2}$

$\frac{2}{3}$

$\frac{3}{4}$

The dark shapes on the stone are all fractions. Match them up to free the spirit of the rocks.

As the last two fractions are matched, the ground beneath Anna's feet begins to tremble, and the stone turns into a huge rock monster. "Do you think he's friendly?" wonders Cleo. In answer, the monster starts to throw numbered rocks at Anna and Cleo. "YOU NOT STEAL GEM!" bellows the creature.

Anna knows how to divide up the rocks to destroy them. She fires a stream of numbers at them, each a factor of one of the monster's numbers. Match the numbers coming from her wand with the rocks. For example, 16 can be exactly divided by 4.

The last rock turns into a blue gem, but as it falls to the ground, it is snatched up by a little blue dragon, who then disappears.

Anna and Cleo race back to the map room. The white dragon is still there, calmly guarding the books.
Cleo gives the dragon a hard stare. "Why did you send us to that dangerous place? I knew we shouldn't have trusted you!"
"The map reveals what it wants to reveal. I have no control over it," replies the dragon. "Perhaps it's showing you where the next theft will happen." Anna consults the map again, and the dragon is right!
It now shows two paths to different rooms.

"Look, Cleo," says Anna. "Which path should we take?"

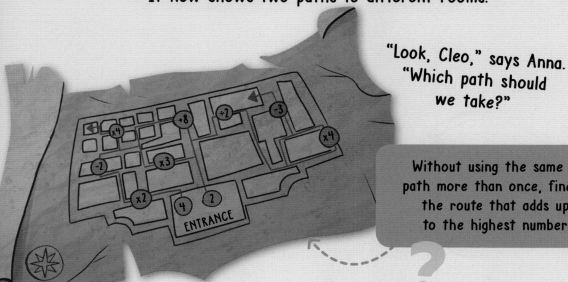

Without using the same path more than once, find the route that adds up to the highest number.

Anna and Cleo follow the route. It leads them up a long staircase to a door that is frozen shut. Anna uses a warming spell to thaw the ice. When the door opens, they are shocked to see a mountain path that leads up to an abandoned temple.

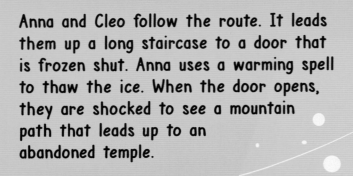

That must be where the gem thief is headed next!

I don't like heights, and I'm not keen on the cold either!

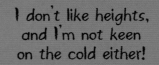

When they get to the temple, the door is padlocked. There is a set of instructions. Which number will the dial point to when the moves are completed?

Turn me 45° as the clock moves, 180° the opposite way, 45° as the clock moves, 90° the opposite way, 180° as the clock moves, 90° as the clock moves.

Inside, the temple is lit by yak-butter candles. It's not abandoned after all! Shivering, Cleo sees a table covered in white fur, and a goblet with a glowing yellow gem on the top. Anna quickly casts a spell upon it. She's not going to lose this one!

Suddenly, there is a roar, and a huge white yeti appears in the doorway.

80.75 6^2 30

8^2 $5\frac{1}{4}$

5.4

$80\frac{1}{2}$ 4^2 15

$\frac{1}{4}$ 0.5

Help Anna cast a weather spell to blow the yeti back outside. Her wand produces a whirlwind of numbers, but they need to be put in order—from low to high. Can you help?

Anna succeeds in sending the yeti away in a blast of wind, but when she turns around, she sees the yellow gem has gone! Cleo is frustrated. "What a useless guardian I am!" she cries. Anna tells her not to worry. "The spell I cast on the gem was a tracking charm. My amulet will lead us to the thief's whereabouts."

To activate the tracking charm, Anna needs to choose the right number from the ring floating around the goblet. Remove all the multiples of 7, all the square numbers, and all the prime numbers. What is left?

The amulet leads the detectives back through the museum, and down to the basement. There are two tunnels to choose from. Eager to prove herself, Cleo races along one toward a light, but Anna's amulet tells her to go down the other tunnel. Reluctantly, she follows Cleo, but the path splits and splits again. It's easy to get lost, and Cleo is nowhere to be seen!

Cleo! Cleo! Where are you?

To find her way back, Anna needs a backward mathmagical spell. Work out what number she began with in this equation: ? x 2 + 2 - 3 = 19.

Back where they started, Anna takes the correct tunnel to follow the stolen gem. She uses her wand to light the way, but fails to notice a trapdoor. Suddenly, she finds herself falling, and lands, slightly bruised, in a secret cellar. The room is lit by a glowing light from a pile of gems. She's found them!

Anna's amulet senses another presence in the room. "Who's there?" she calls. Perhaps she can use one of the gems to cast a revealing spell. The gem she needs has a number that is made by multiplying together the numbers on two other gems. Can you see it?

3
6
9   12
16   24
26   29
32   40
38   42
48
55

As she reaches to pick it up, an enormous dragon reveals itself. "Thank you," it says. "Without you and your sphinx, I would never have been able to collect those last two gems!" The dragon steps aside to reveal the tiny sphinx imprisoned in a cage.
"Cleo!" cries Anna. "So, all those little dragons were working for you!" she says to the giant monster.
The dragon laughs. "Working for me? They are all part of me!"

"Let me out, you thieving dragon!" demands Cleo. Anna raises her wand to free Cleo, but the huge dragon is too strong for her magic.

Without warning, the dragon breathes a jet of fire! Can you help Anna to turn away the flames, by completing these division equations?

$44 \div ? = 4$

$48 \div ? = 6$

$35 \div ? = 5$

$27 \div ? = 9$

$42 \div ? = 7$

$36 \div ? = 3$

"Your mathmagic won't protect you, little one," grins the giant creature. "Don't you like my gem collection? It lights up my lair."
"I don't like thieves!" says brave Anna. "Especially big monster thieves!"
"I am not a monster," says the dragon. "I will strike you a deal. If you can solve this puzzle, I shall let you live."

Look at this collection of gems. Find one with more than four sides and fewer than eight. It must touch more than two gems but not one with eight sides.

When Anna chooses the correct gem, the dragon simply smiles.
"Two lives, two puzzles, or have you forgotten little Cleo?"
The dragon sets another number puzzle.

You meanie!

Look at the 60 gems on the dragon's wing. What percentage of them are blue? What percentage are pink? What percentage are oval? Work out the answers to save Cleo.

Anna gets it right again, and the dragon agrees to let them live, but says they can never leave his dark cellar! "I cannot have you telling anyone about these gems," it says. "They are all that light my lonely prison."

"Prison?" asks Anna. "But can't you divide and escape as smaller dragons anytime you want?"

"Alas, no. I can only free one part of myself at a time. I was trapped here in the darkness thousands of years ago by a wizard. That's why I collect the gems."

"What if I could promise you a light that is brighter than all your gems put together?" asks Anna.

"If you could bring me that, of course I would free you," says the dragon.

To deliver on that promise, Anna works out how bright all of the dragon's gems are. 30% of the light in the cellar is produced by 60 pink gems, 25% by 100 blue gems, 20% by 80 yellow gems, and the rest by 250 other gems. What percentage of the light is produced by each kind of gem?

Anna tells Cleo to help with the magic by closing her eyes and imagining a bright yellow gem. Anna reaches into a pocket and pulls out a pair of shades as she says a powerful magic word.

4 15 22 18 24 7 12 15 4

21 ÷ 3 = I, 11 x 2 = L, 4 x 6 = M, 36 ÷ 3 = N, 29 – 14 = O,
44 ÷ 11 = S, and 6 x 3 = U.
What is the magic word?

The spell creates a hole in the ceiling that lets a stream of bright sunlight into the cellar. The light reflects off the gems, temporarily blinding the dragon, and allowing Anna to free Cleo. But the dragon's reaction is a surprise to Anna. Tears spring to its eyes.

"Thank you," it says. "I have spent so long trapped in the dark trying to bring a little light to it, I had forgotten the beauty of sunlight." "Anna?" cautions Cleo. "You're not thinking of freeing this huge, thieving dragon, are you?" The dragon overhears her. "All I want," sighs the dragon, "is to live peacefully, and watch the sun rise every morning. I'll give back all the magical gems for that."

To avoid any magical accidents, the gems must be collected into groups that add up to 50, before they are returned to the museum. Red gems equal 20, blue 10, pink 5, and yellow 2. Each group must have at least one of each kind of gem. What combination of gems should each group have?

To help the dragon split into five smaller dragons and release him from the prison, Anna needs a very special division spell.

1

5

12

16

20

24

32

35

4

2

3

72   80

42   58

50   60

Help Anna choose the one number that is exactly divisible by all the numbers on the dragons.

59

Once the dragon is freed, Anna finds a home for it in a cave on a high mountain, where it can watch the sunrise every day. Back in the museum, the stolen gems have been returned, and Cleo is asked whether or not she will return to being a stone guardian. "I've been doing that job for over 2,000 years," she claims, "and I wasn't really that good at it!"

Could I join you on your magical adventures instead? That seems much more fun than sitting still for millennia.

Anna agrees to train Cleo as her mathmagical assistant, and new adventures await!

Cleo chooses a magic wand to begin her mathmagical training. Each has a number. The number of the wand she chooses is exactly divisible by 3, and it can be found by taking away one wand number from another. Which is it?

HALEY COMET AND THE CALCULON CRISIS

MEET HALEY COMET AND THE MATHSTRONAUTS

When colonies on distant worlds are threatened by the Calculons, there's one team that the Earth Space Service (E.S.S.) trust to keep the peace.

HALEY COMET

Captain Haley Comet is a pioneer, the first pilot to steer through hyperspace, and a veteran of the Algebra War. Signing up for the Space Service in her teens, she was soon promoted to captain of the Pythagoras.

TURNER NORTH

Turner North is a new recruit to the Space Service but he's already proved himself an excellent navigator. He's half-Altaran—the top half—with a secret talent.

STELLA SPARK

Stella Spark is Haley's second-in-command and the ship's chief engineer. She knows the Pythagoras like the back of her hand, which is usually dirty with engine grease.

Haley Comet is busy fighting off an invasion of building-munching megabats when the call comes through. "Urgent message from the Space Service, Captain!" says the young recruit carrying the comms tablet.

Take over from me!

Highly sensitive, the message is in code. Some letters from the message are replaced with numbers. Work out the missing letters from the clues,
A = 4 x 2, C = 10 - 8, E = 2 x 2, L = 2 ÷ 2, T = 8 - 2.

8SS4MB14
2R4W 86
18UN2H
20N6R01
RIGH6
8W8Y

At Launch Control, Haley, chief engineer Stella Spark, and navigator Turner North receive the report from Admiral Yu. "The peace treaty with the Calculons is under threat," he says.

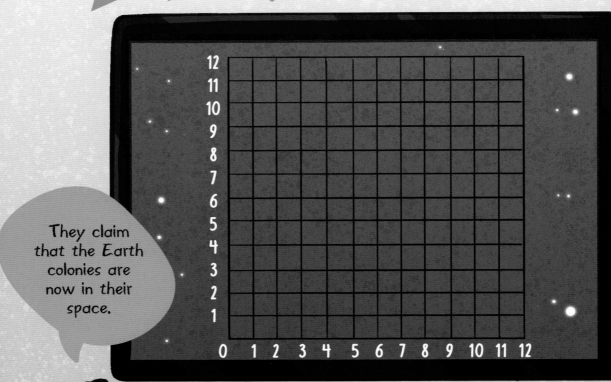

They claim that the Earth colonies are now in their space.

According to the Calculons, Earth's colonies are at the following coordinates on the star map. Read first by column, then by row:
2,10 ; 3,10 ; 5,9 ; 8,1 ; 8,6.
Now draw an arc to show the border of Calculon space.
4,8 ; 5,5 ; 5,11 ; 6,4 ; 8,3 ; 10,3.
Are there Earth colonies in Calculon space, on the right of the arc?

Stella Spark needs to get the E.S.S. Pythagoras ready to head to the first world threatened—Earth Colony Alpha. She has made a few improvements to the ship since their last mission.

How many fuel rods does Stella need aboard ship for the mission? If a journey of 30 light years requires 40 fuel rods, how many are needed for a journey of 24 light years?

With the starship prepared for launch, Haley steps forward to give a speech. "Guys, this could be our most important mission yet. We don't know much about the Calculons. They have lived quietly alongside us for decades. If we don't handle the situation carefully, we could end up in an interstellar war! Now, prepare for launch!"

Turner North turns to Stella and asks, "Are Captain Comet's missions always this risky?"

"Most days," says Stella, heading to the engine room. "You get used to it."

Turner gulps and checks his navigation plan for the zillionth time.

Help Turner with his navigation plan. Starting with the number 10, find a route to Earth Colony Alpha, putting the number through all the calculations without crossing your path. Which route results in the lowest figure?

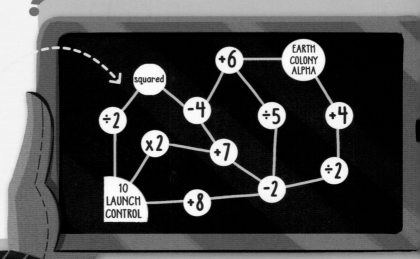

It's take-off, and the team says goodbye to the Solar System.
"Back to eating starship rations," moans Stella.
"You like Earth food?" asks Turner. "On my father's planet, we eat delicious giant millipedes." "But aren't you only half-alien?" asks Stella.
"Yes," says Turner, "So I eat the millipedes with fries."
Haley interrupts the pair's chatter.

Time to engage the hyperdrive!

4, 7, 10, 5, 3, 8, 12, 6, 9, 100

To engage the hyperdrive you must replace all the numbers on the control screen with their squares.

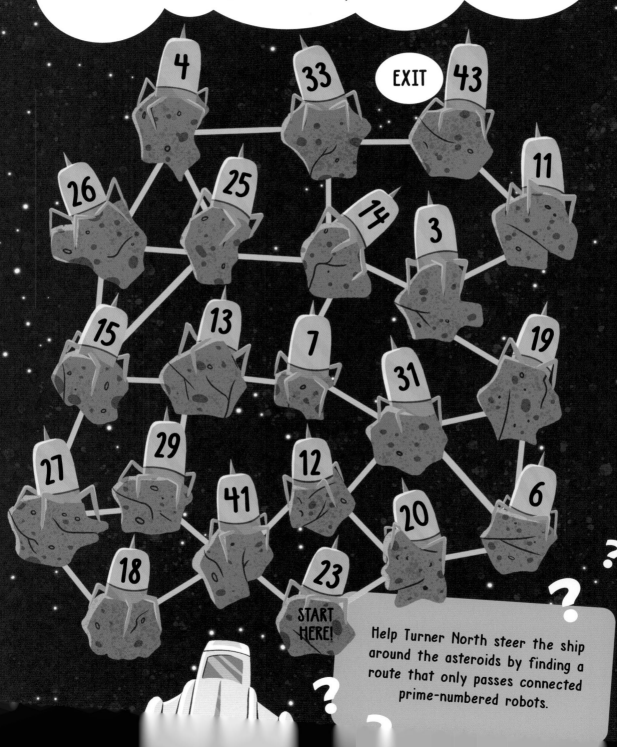

Finally, the heroes arrive at Earth Colony Alpha and hear the dangerous demands made by the Calculons. "The Calculons gave us just five months to leave or else," says the Colony Leader. "They said they would move our planet out of Calculon space, really close to one of our suns!"

You've lived on this planet for decades. Why have the Calculons decided you are in their space now?

DISTANCE FROM SUNS

Look at the chart for the position of Earth Colony Alpha near the suns. The colonists can survive in a zone that is 25% nearer or 25% farther away than now. Can their planet be safely moved into point "X?"

Suddenly and without warning, a Calculon army arrives! "They're too soon!" shouts the Colony Leader. The Calculons have sent a squadron of Genisects—giant, mutated insects—to clear the colony before the planet is relocated. "There must be something wrong with their calendars as well as their maps!" says Stella.

Have the Calculons made a mistake? They gave the colonists a deadline of five months, and waited 120 days. One Earth year is based on one orbit of the Sun: 365 days. The colonists' world takes 65 fewer days to go around its suns, and their year is divided into 12 equal months.

The Genisects have been instructed to stun the Earth colonists with their insect stingers, and round them up with webbing. Genisects have different numbers of legs. Haley and her team use laser lassos to stop them.

Round them up! Don't harm any of them!

10 Genisects have 8 legs, 9 have 4 legs, 5 have 12. Each laser lasso can tie up 4 legs. How many lassos are needed to stop the Genisects?

With the Genisects safely captured, Haley decides she must meet the Calculons face to face, but before she can get her crew to the *Pythagoras*, the Calculons' ship departs.
"That's that then," says Stella. "No one knows the way to Calculus, their home planet!"
"I disagree," says Turner watching the ship depart through his technoculars. He leads Haley and Stella back to the *Pythagoras* to show them how to track the alien ship.

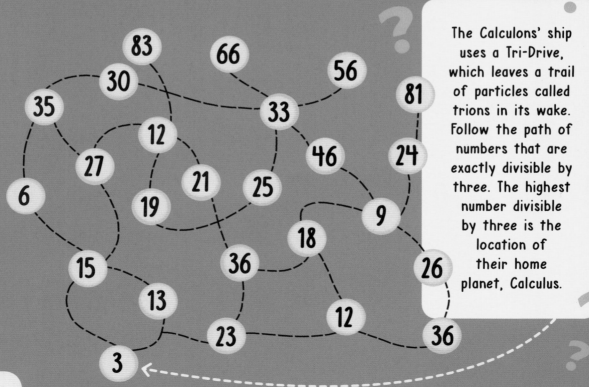

The Calculons' ship uses a Tri-Drive, which leaves a trail of particles called trions in its wake. Follow the path of numbers that are exactly divisible by three. The highest number divisible by three is the location of their home planet, Calculus.

On the way to Calculus, the *Pythagoras* voyages into unknown space.
Suddenly the ship's alarm goes off.
"Red Alert! Red Alert! Unknown space anomaly ahead!"
Stella checks her scanners. "It's a huge cloud of gas that feeds on passing debris, and it's trying to suck us in!" she says.
"We're doomed!" cries Turner.
"Wait a sec," says Stella. "My scanner says it's feasting on prime numbers."

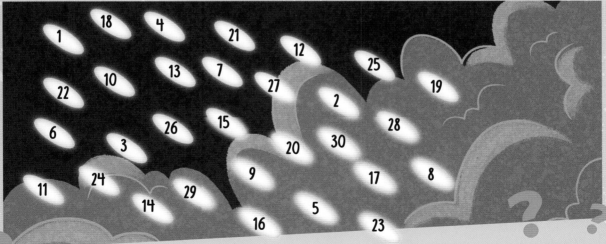

To avoid being sucked in, Haley's team must fire photon beams of different wavelengths at the anomaly to "feed" it. Choose the 10 beams marked with prime numbers.

Finally the heroes reach the planet Calculus, where they receive a message over the ship's comm. "Earthlings! You are trespassing in Calculon space, and face arrest."

"I was hoping for a friendlier welcome!" says Haley.

The ship comes to a juddering halt. "We're caught in a graviton ray!" says Stella, boosting the engines to try to pull free.

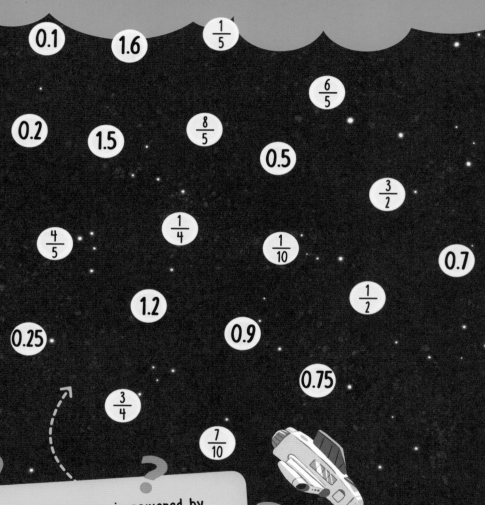

0.1 1.6 $\frac{1}{5}$

$\frac{6}{5}$

0.2 1.5 $\frac{8}{5}$

0.5

$\frac{3}{2}$

$\frac{4}{5}$ $\frac{1}{4}$ $\frac{1}{10}$

0.7

1.2 $\frac{1}{2}$

0.25 0.9

0.75

$\frac{3}{4}$

$\frac{7}{10}$

The graviton ray is powered by fractions. All but one of the decimals "neutralizes" one of the fractions. Can you find the decimal that doesn't?

Despite Stella's best efforts, the E.S.S. *Pythagoras* is dragged to a Calculus docking bay. Haley orders her crew to offer no resistance as they are brought to meet the leader of the Calculons. Turner is astonished. "The head of the Calculons is... a huge head!" he says.
Indeed, the leader of the Calculons is a large head in a tank. The head is connected by tubes that keep him alive and help him talk. "I know why you are here," says the Head. "But I won't change my mind. Your colonies are in Calculon space and must be removed." As the Head speaks, his calculations are seen on a huge screen. "This is my proof," he says.

$$15 \div 3 + 5 = 0$$
$$4 + 12 - 8 = 40$$
$$6 \times 10 \div 2 = 8,$$
$$40 - 15 - 5 = 5$$
$$32 - 4 - 6 = 2$$
$$9 \times 3 \times 5 = 32$$

There is something wrong with all the Head's calculations. Replace just one symbol in each calculation to make the equations work.

The Head has got a problem with his mathematics, and Haley and her team wonder how to raise the subject.

Before they can speak, the Head reveals more of his plans. "Once we have removed the nearest colony world, we can move to the next planet in our space..."

The name of the planet on the chart is in code, with each number representing a letter.

$$100 \div 20$$
$$0.5 \times 2$$
$$50 - 32$$
$$40 \times \tfrac{1}{2}$$
$$56 \div 7$$

Help Haley work out the name of the planet. Each number matches a letter of the alphabet. A = 1, B = 2, C = 3, and so on.

Haley tries to negotiate, but she fails, and the trio are put in a cell.
"Could this mission get any worse?" moans Turner.
"We haven't tasted Calculon food yet!" Stella jokes.
"I'll have you know, Calculon food is renowned," says a voice
from outside the cell. A Calculon woman in a long robe appears.
"I am Glatina, advisor to the Head."
"Nice to meet you," Haley replies, "Now could you advise
the Head that his mathematics are all wrong!"
Glatina sighs. "I know. His equations have been getting worse
for months, but no one dares question him."
"Can you warn Earth of the problem?" asks Haley.
Before leaving, Glatina gives the prisoners a clue to help
them escape. "Tell no one I have helped you," she says.

Glatina tells Haley that the cell's door
code is the next five numbers in
the sequence 4, 6, 9, 13, 18.
What is the code?

The team escape their cell and sneak past a guard. Now they have to translate an alien map to find their way through the capital city.
"We have to free the *Pythagoras* from the graviton ray," says Turner.
"I can deal with the graviton ray," says Stella Spark,
"if I can gain access to the city's main computer terminal."

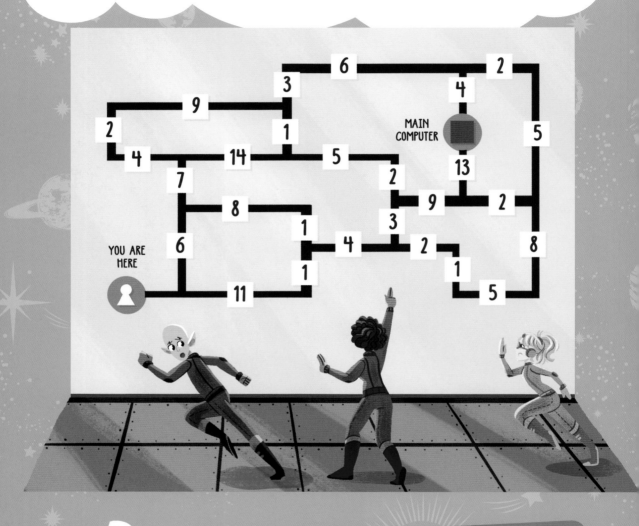

The map of the Calculon city shows travel times in calcuminutes for various routes. Each path is numbered along its length. Which is the fastest route to the main computer?

The alarms go off—the heroes' escape has been discovered.
"It won't be long till they find us!" says Turner.
Stella tells him to calm down. "I have an idea." She plugs her translator earpiece into a communications terminal. "If I change the alarm signal to a radiation alert, the guards will run away from us, instead of toward us! I may be able to clear our route..."

To change the alarm to a radiation alert, Stella must replace all the even numbers in the problems (before the equals sign) with the next odd number up. What will be the new solutions?

$$8 \times 6 = 48$$
$$28 - 16 = 12$$
$$24 + 8 + 4 = 36$$
$$20 \div 2 = 10$$
$$10 \times 4 = 40$$

The trio reach the main computer room, which is guarded by a security team. Spotting a service robot nearby, Turner North reveals a hidden talent. "There's something you might not know about my father's race, Altaran. They can change their appearance..."

"So I've heard," says Haley.

"But I am only half Altaran," Turner explains. "I can only change my top half." Turner transforms his upper half to look like the service robot, and borrows its garbage container. "Hop in!" says Turner. It's smelly, but Haley and Stella hide inside it, so Turner can wheel them past the guards and into the computer room.

Unlock the computer room door by completing all the calculations in the grid. The code numbers are on the white tiles.

$$\square \times 6 - 11 = 7$$
$$\square \times \square \div 3 = \square$$
$$18 \quad \square + \square = 28$$
$$\square \times 18 = 36$$

Just as Turner expected, there are operators inside the computer room.
"Did you not get the orders?" asks Turner in a robotic voice.
"The room must be fumigated. You will have to leave immediately,
and don't come back for an hour!"
The operators leave without questions.
Now Stella and Haley can get out of the smelly garbage container.
Stella sets to work, freeing their ship from the graviton ray.

$$\frac{1}{5} \quad \frac{1}{100} \quad \frac{3}{2} \quad \frac{1}{10}$$

$$\frac{1}{4} \quad \frac{3}{5} \quad \frac{4}{5} \quad \frac{1}{2} \quad \frac{1}{25} \quad \frac{3}{4}$$

80%   50%   1%   25%   150%
20%   4%   60%   10%   75%

The graviton ray is powered by fractions. Help Stella match
the fractions with percentages to turn off the ray.

Stella succeeds in deactivating the graviton ray, and returns with Haley to hide in the garbage container, so they can sneak out. Once out of sight of guards and cameras, Turner changes back to his regular form, while Haley and Stella climb out again—they smell pretty bad! "Lucky I don't have a sense of smell!" jokes Turner, but Haley and Stella fail to see the funny side. Haley checks a computer display. "Our ship is docked at Bay 42," she says. "That's where we need to be."

To reach Bay 42, the trio must follow a number-sequence route. Which sequence leads to 42? Continue the sequences on the display to find out.

The trio arrive at Bay 42, and find a group of Calculons fleeing in the opposite direction. Haley looks through a window and sees why. "The *Pythagoras* is trying to pull away from a docking clamp," she says. "Without the graviton ray to hold the ship in position, its engines are pulling against it."
"We must move fast before the clamp or ship are torn apart!" warns Stella. The crew hurries to board the ship.

Stella must rearrange the numbers on the ship's four engines, so they produce equal results. Swap one number from each engine with one from another engine, so all four give the same total.

A.
8
9   1

B.
6
10   5

C.
10
15   4

D.
8
21   3

Haley's team manages to bring the E.S.S. *Pythagoras* under control and free it from the docking clamp, but the clamp is damaged and leans toward the government building. It could fall at any second. Haley uses a jetpack to hurry over and evacuate the hall.

There are four rooms to evacuate and 80 Calculons. 50% of them are in Room A, 20% in room B, 25% in Room C, and the rest in Room D. How many Calculons are in each room?

Danger! The towering docking clamp topples over and smashes into the government hall. Haley manages to help everyone out except the Head. He's stuck in his giant tank with the clamp leaning on top! Haley calls Turner and Stella for help. Stella must use her engineering skills to build a buttress with a girder to hold up the clamp.

Help Stella form a right-angled triangle with the girder. If the triangle's width is 5 calculengths and its height is 12 calculengths, how long should the girder be? The square of the longest side is equal to the squares of the two shorter sides, added together. "This is really tough!" says Stella.

Before the team can save the tank, a crack forms, and it begins to leak. The trio rushes to help free the Head as the water gushes out.
"He's not a head after all!" says Turner. Indeed, the glass and water in the tank magnified his head so much that it hid his body!

The tank is 10 x 15 x 10 calculengths. How many cubic calculengths of liquid does it contain?

Released from the tank, the Head admits he is tired of complicated equations. "It's time for me to retire," he says.

Stepping outside the hall, he gathers his advisors about him.

"Glatina," he calls. "I select you to be my replacement."

Glatina steps forward, astonished at the offer, but proud.

"I will gladly take charge," she says. "But no more tanks, and, from now on, there must be a council of mathematicians to check all my equations!"

The first thing on Glatina's list is to correct all of the Head's mistakes, and secure Earth's colonies.

$$3 \times ? \times 2 = 30$$
$$7 \times 2 + ? = 20$$
$$100 \div ? - 8 = 12$$
$$14 \times 2 + ? = 62$$
$$8 \times 6 - ? = 23$$
$$13 + ? - 20 = 13$$

Help Glatina fix all of the calculations by putting the right number in each empty space.

With Calculus under new leadership, and the Earth colonies safe once more, Haley and her crew head back to Earth, where they are hailed as heroes. As a reward, the trio are presented with a new starship, the E.S.S. *Fibonacci*.

Congratulations!

	E.S.S. *PYTHAGORAS*	PERCENTAGE INCREASE	E.S.S. *FIBONACCI*
Speed	12	25%	
Power	40	20%	
Mass	2,000	10%	
Length	300	5%	
Crew quarters	8	75%	

The new ship is an upgrade of the E.S.S. *Pythagoras*. Look at the percentage improvements to work out the new ratings for the *Fibonacci*.

THE MYSTERIOUS CITY OF EL NUMERO

Meet Daring Explorers Daisy and Dale Deed

When sister and brother Daisy and Dale Deed receive a gift from their missing father, it leads them on a journey over rough seas, to face hair-raising tests that will solve the mystery of El Numero.

Siblings Daisy and Dale Deed are wiser than their young years might suggest. After their mother passed away, their father, the historian and adventurer Professor Darren Deed, raised them on his own. He taught them ancient history, geography, and mathematics, until he left on a mission to South America, and was never seen again.

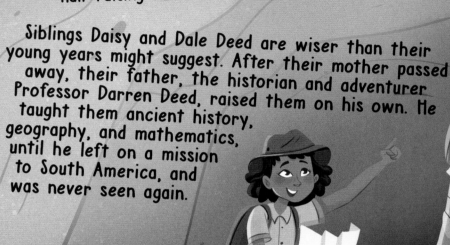

DAISY DEED

DALE DEED

CAPTAIN CAMILA

Captain Camila is a brave sea captain and old friend of Professor Deed. Famed for her solo crossing of the infamous Suicide Straits, she retired from competitive yacht racing to work as a skipper for hire in the notorious port of Santa Luna.

A year after their father's disappearance, Daisy and Dale receive a mysterious parcel in the mail. Hurriedly unwrapping it, they find a pocket watch inside. "Didn't this belong to Dad?" asks Dale.
"I think there's something inside it!" says Daisy, struggling with the clasp.
"Give it here—I'll do it," says Dale. However, he soon gives up, looking red-faced. Daisy bursts out laughing.
Then Dale remembers something. "The portrait!" In the living room of their home hangs a painting, showing their dad holding the very same watch. "There's the watch—and there are three clocks, too!"

I think there's a clue to opening it in the painting.

That would be typical of Dad!

"The title of the painting is 'From Noon Till Night.'" says Daisy. "Perhaps we should turn the hands on the watch to point to the four times in the painting, in the the right order." Can you help them?

With the correct turns, the watch cover pops open. There aren't any cogs inside. Instead it holds a folded, hand-drawn map. The map shows the location of a mysterious South American island, El Numero. Dale tries to look it up in an atlas, but the island doesn't seem to exist!

Could Dad have made a mistake?

Each square on the map represents 4 nautical miles. Prof Deed's notes say El Numero is 12 nautical miles west of Devil's Deep, 8 nautical miles toward Wreckage Reef, 8 nautical miles farther west, then 20 nautical miles north. Reading first by column, then by row, at what coordinates should El Numero be found?

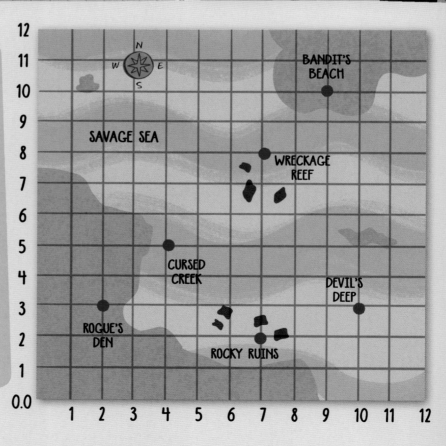

The island of El Numero is not marked on the map,
but Daisy and Dale decide to look for it anyway.

Having raised the money for flights and boat hire, the siblings head to the airport and look at the schedules.

FROM	TO	LEAVING	FLIGHT TIME
Townton	Miami	8:30am	6 hours
Miami	Star City		4½ hours
Star City	Santa Luna		2 hours

We need to catch these three connecting flights to reach Santa Luna.

Santa Luna is eight hours ahead of Townton, where they are setting out from. If they have one hour between each flight landing and the next taking off, what will the local time be when they arrive in Santa Luna?

Daisy and Dale arrive at Santa Luna, feeling very tired! They are met by a blue-eyed man who claims to be the boat captain they hired. He offers them a lift to the dock where his boat is moored.

Do any of the boats at the dock have a number to match Daisy's description?

Assuming it's their mistake, Dale and Daisy get aboard the blue-eyed man's boat. Some way out to sea, he demands their map.
"I'll take that as my payment for your safe voyage," he says, "That is, unless you'd rather get off here!"
"There are sharks! We'd get eaten alive!" cries Dale.
"Don't worry," says the captain. "I'll restore the map to its owners."

I am a guardian of the sacred island of El Numero. No strangers are allowed there! I have been guarding the island since I was 18. My father, too. He was guardian for 37 years before me. I am 43 now. In ten years' time I will pass my father's record.

Check the captain's mathematics. Is he telling the truth?

Daisy and Dale take their chances in the sea. Luckily, the sharks turn out to be dolphins! As the captain's boat sails out of view, a second boat appears, and the Deeds wave to get its attention. Getting alongside, the captain of the new boat helps them aboard. "Strange place to go for a swim," she jokes. Daisy gives the captain a hard stare and grabs a towel. "We were forced into the water by our captain," she says. "That wasn't your captain," says the boatswoman. "I am." She introduces herself as Captain Camila. "I was late reaching the airport, and couldn't stop that villain leading you away. I gave chase in my boat."

Dale explains their plan. "I've heard legends of El Numero and its countless treasures," says Captain Camila. "It's said to be in the Savage Sea, but too many ships have been wrecked there." Camila shows her new passengers a chart.

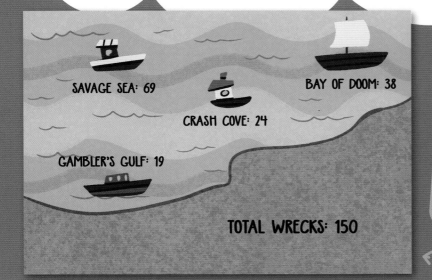

SAVAGE SEA: 69

CRASH COVE: 24

BAY OF DOOM: 38

GAMBLER'S GULF: 19

TOTAL WRECKS: 150

Look at the chart for the accidents in the local seas. What percentage of the accidents happened in the Savage Sea?

"Your father tried to hire me for this same voyage," says Camila. "You knew our dad?" asks Dale. Camila nods. "He contacted me a week before he disappeared. I'll help you find the island, and hopefully your father, too. But first we need a course..."
Daisy and Dale try to remember enough details to get them to the island.

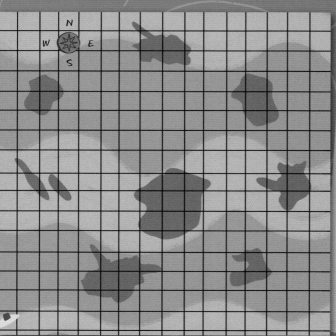

Work out the destination on the map from their start point. The boat heads north for 3 hours, then east for 1½ hours, turning south for ¼ hour, then east for 2 hours, then north for 1 hour, then west for ¼ hour. Each map square is 4 knots across. If the boat sails at exactly 16 knots an hour, where will it end up on the map?

The going is good for a while, before the boat enters rough seas and the hull hits a rock, springing a leak. While the captain hurries to make a repair, Daisy and Dale need to bail out water.

Faster! Faster!

Water is getting into the boat at a rate of 4 cups a second. Each bucket can hold 10 cups. How many buckets of water must the kids bail from the boat every minute to stop the situation getting worse?

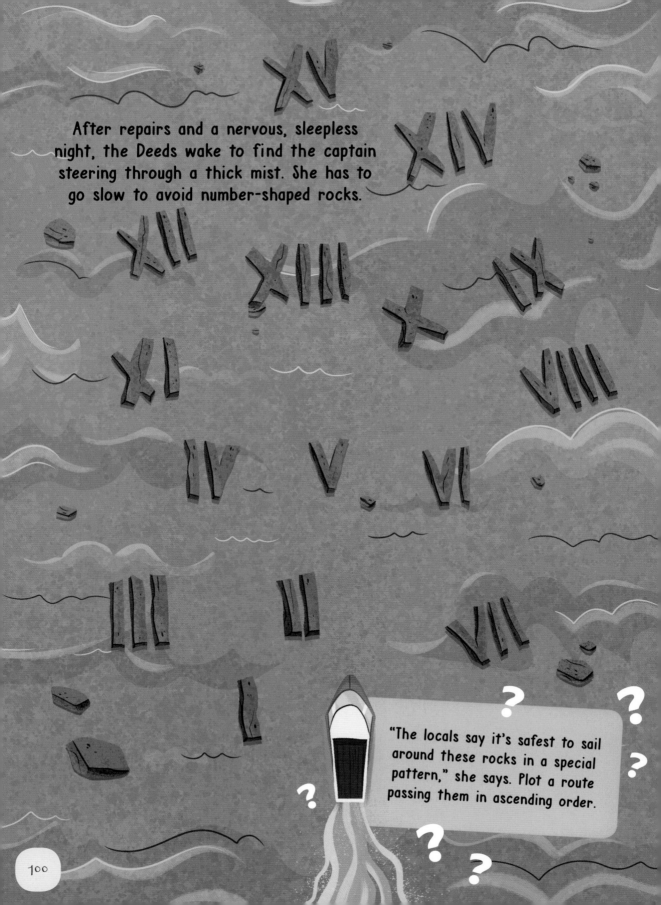

After repairs and a nervous, sleepless night, the Deeds wake to find the captain steering through a thick mist. She has to go slow to avoid number-shaped rocks.

"The locals say it's safest to sail around these rocks in a special pattern," she says. Plot a route passing them in ascending order.

Suddenly, there is a bump, but it's not a rock they've hit. Daisy and Dale look over the side of the boat. "It's wreckage!" says Dale. Daisy recognizes it. "It's what's left of that mean sailor's boat—the one who stole our map!" "Serves him right!" says Dale, though he is glad there is no sign of the blue-eyed man.

Then, a spooky island appears in front of them, emerging from the fog. Camila steers the boat around the coastline to find a safe place to weigh anchor.

Land ahoy!

The island has a coastline that is 200 boat lengths long with 40 boat lengths of cliffs, 30 boat lengths of jagged rocks, 80 boat lengths surrounded by reefs, and the rest by beaches. What percentage of the coast is beach?

Mooring off a beach, the trio begin exploring the island. There are pawprints on a path, perhaps belonging to some savage animal, but there's no other route, so they follow. Without weapons, Captain Camila arms herself with a flare pistol.

There are numbered stakes along the way, leading in different directions. Each bears a skull with a painted number. Many skulls are fanged. It feels like a warning. Dale points out that, while some skulls face toward them, others face stakes farther ahead on the path.

They are following a number sequence!

The first numbers in the sequence are 1, 2, 4, 7, 11. What is the pattern, and what four numbers come next?

The stakes lead to the entrance of a dark cave. Camila tries to rub sticks together to make a flame, but the wood is too damp, and she isn't very good at it. "I'm a sailor!" she laments. The trio prepare to enter the darkness using touch to find their way.

Painted on the cave entrance are symbols that might help guide them. The symbols are images of feet pointing in different directions—ahead, left, right, and back. Each foot has a number on it. "I think these show the number of steps we should take in each direction," says Daisy.

The feet show steps in the following directions: 6 Ahead, 3 Right, 4 Ahead, 2 Left, 3 Back, 1 Left, 5 Ahead, 2 Right, 2 Back, 1 Left, 5 Ahead. Simplify the route so you can reach the end point by moving just ahead, then right. How many steps need they take in each direction?

As they feel their way in the darkness, they hear growling that makes them shiver. They recall the footprints and skulls. Daisy reminds Camila of her flare gun. The captain nods in the dark and replies, "Close your eyes for a second." She fires the flare into the darkness, and glimpses an animal as it runs away down a side tunnel. She also spies a wooden door just ahead. When they get near, Camila says, "There's one lock but eight keys! Which one do we use?"

Daisy has an answer. "We need to use all eight, but in the right order!"

START LOW 🔑 GO HIGH

2.2 2^2 0.5   0.25   1/3   4.5   5/4   1.2

The door has one lock but eight keys. The keys are numbered with decimals and fractions. To open the door, they need to use the keys in the order from the lowest number to the highest. What is the order?

The door is opened and the trio gasp. They are inside a high-ceilinged, candlelit room, decorated with carvings, paintings, and tapestries covered in numbers, symbols, and equations. They now know for sure they are within the walls of the Temple of El Numero. The path ahead is over numbered hexagonal stones. Dale shrieks. Next to the path is a skeleton. "It looks like he's been dead for a very long time!" Daisy says. "The skeleton is pointing ahead to the number 108, but why that number?"

Dale is less scared now.
He sees a pattern...

The skeleton points to the number 108. Follow the times table that includes this number, stepping only on touching stones.

We need to start from the first number in that times table.

To double-check the route, Daisy throws Dale's backpack onto the first stone. "Hey, my snacks are in there!" he complains. The stone proves safe to stand on, and the trio step gingerly ahead. Suddenly, Captain Camila is spooked by a bat swooping down from the ceiling. She accidentally steps back onto one of the unsafe stones, and her foot becomes trapped in a hidden mechanism. A crackling, pre-recorded voice echoes around the chamber. "You have 10 seconds to escape this room, before you are trapped." "Quickly," shouts Daisy, "Run for it!"

Camila needs help to free her foot—and it will take 2.5 seconds to release it. Dale can run 4 paces each second, and is 12 paces from Camila. Daisy can run five paces each second, and is 20 paces from Camila. Because she is limping, Camila runs half as fast as Daisy. She is 10 paces from the exit. Can they all escape in time?

80

56

45

81

On the other side of the door is a long corridor. Dale hears a growling sound behind them, so they pick up the pace. They dash through another door, but this one seems to be stuck in the open position! How can they close it before the creature catches up?

Lock the door quickly!

How?

The door closes by the use of weights. There are three balances beside the door, with different combinations of stones. How many stones from the pile are needed to balance the bottom set?

With the balance set, the door closes behind them. They hear a new sound in the chamber—a voice crying out from a cage in the corner. It's the captain who stole the map. He must have swum to the island after his boat sank. Seeing Daisy and Dale, he pleads to be freed. "I'm sorry I left you in the sea. I'm happy to see you alive," he says. "If you set me free, I can give you a clue to getting farther into the temple." Reluctantly, Daisy and Dale agree. To do so, they need to unlock his cage.

The door is operated with four sliding latches. How should Daisy and Dale position the latches so the equation running down the middle will make 13 become 63?

13

+	−	X
2	5	8
−	X	÷
2	3	5

= 63

As soon as he is released, the captain runs toward the exit, opening the door to flee. Seconds later, there is a bang and a crash, but the Deeds and Captain Camila decide not to investigate.
They lock the door again and proceed deeper into El Numero.
They enter a corridor with a series of statues along one wall.
Each statue is from a different age.

The first statue is dated 2673. The final one is dated 3761.
How many years are there between them?
2019 is 3761 in the El Numero calendar, what year was 2673?

The kids now know that El Numero is much older than they thought. What is its purpose? They enter a large echoing chamber with columns, a gallery, and hanging braziers, decorated with numbers and equations, many far beyond Daisy and Dale's knowledge of mathematics. Dale is about to speak when Daisy tells him to shush. They hear footsteps coming from the corridor behind them ... and growling! The beast is still tracking them. Dale spots a large closet they may be able to hide inside.

Opening the lock on the closet requires a series of turns, first one way, then the other. What position will it be in once all the turns are followed?

The trio opens the closet, but it is too full of ceremonial gowns to squeeze into. The creature has them cornered! Suddenly they hear: "Digit! Leave!" Revealed in the light, the creature is a dog. It trots over to its master, who steps out from the shadows. "Dad!" cry the children. Indeed, it is Professor Deed, now with a beard. He hugs them and thanks Captain Camila.

"This is Digit," says the professor, pointing to the dog.
It licks the children's hands.

"You shouldn't have followed me," he tells his kids. "It's not safe!"
"Then why did you leave us a clue?" asks Daisy.
"I wanted you to know I was alive," says her father,
"not risk all to rescue me." He reveals how he found El Numero,
by drawing a diagram on the dusty floor.

The professor had unearthed an ancient tile with five numbers missing. These were map distances. All the rows and columns and diagonals of three squares in the square should add up to 15. What are the missing numbers?

While happy to be reunited with his children, the professor looks sad, and reveals the reason why. "I'm so relieved to see you," he says, "but they won't let me leave." He unbuttons his shirt to reveal a talisman around his neck. The symbols on the talisman add up to a secret number, the number that means he must remain.

What is the professor's number? It's represented by the letter "N" in all the clues.

$N < 4^2$
$N > 3^2$
N is odd.
$N < 3 \times 5$
$N > XI$

The head guardian of El Numero enters the room and greets the professor by his number. He turns to the new arrivals. "You passed the number tests to enter El Numero," he says. "Well done!" The kids smile, but then the guardian says, "Now you must all remain here... forever!" Captain Camila quickly grabs the children and tries to escape, but the exit is blocked by guards.

"The outside world can never learn the secrets of El Numero," says the guardian. The family and Captain Camila are led into the main council chamber, where 11 other guardians are assembled. The head explains that El Numero was built to protect the ancient mathematics, to ensure numbers always add up to the same results.

"Don't they always add up to the same results?" wonders Dale, but Daisy nudges him to be quiet. She doesn't want them to get into more trouble.

I am the 22nd head guardian, in my final year. Since El Numero was built, every head guardian has spent exactly 50 years keeping El Numero secret.

How many years is it since El Numero was built?

Since ancient times, the guardians of El Numero have formed a Prime Number Council of 13. When Professor Deed happened upon the island they had just lost one member. The professor agreed to remain. "I wasn't given a choice!" whispered the professor to his children. Daisy looked thoughtful, then spoke up.

If prime numbers are important, why not form two Prime Number Councils, using a total of 12 members instead of 13, so my father could go free?

How can 12 be split into two prime numbers?

The guardians mutter to each other, then agree to this revolutionary idea—perhaps they should consider inviting youngsters to join their council! The kids worry they will be forced to stay after all, but the head guardian agrees to free their father from his duties.

With your father free to watch over you, I trust you, and the boat captain, to swear an oath never to reveal details of El Numero.

The oath the visitors must swear is a mathematical promise. They must remove four numbers from those chosen by the guardian to leave a total of 50. Which four numbers do they remove from 3, 8, 11, 15, 23, 31, 33?

ANSWERS

CHAPTER 1

PAGE 7
650

PAGE 8
13 is not exactly divisible by 3.
9, 6, 5, 4

PAGE 9
40

PAGE 10
The first row shows square numbers: 1, 4, 9, 16, 25, 36, 49.

Each number in the second row is made by adding together the previous two: 1, 1, 2, 3, 5, 8, 13, 21.

The third row is the nine times table backward: 81, 72, 63, 54, 45, 36, 27.

PAGE 11
Prime Plaza, 4 x 16 = 64
Sky View, 4 x 14 = 56
Super Block, 5 x 9 = 45
Power Tower is the target, 6 x 8 = 48.

PAGE 12
Route marked in pink, below:

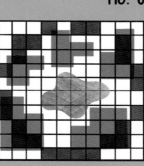

63
31
45
12
28 9 47 30
16 97 2 94
72 96 73 54
44 32 87
36 91 48 70
55 21
33 52
79 50 14
41 84
83 67 72
29 85 54
12 7 72 10

PAGE 13
The pairs that add up to 100 are: 9-91, 10-90, 15-85, 18-82, 23-77, 29-71, 33-67, 37-63, 45-55, and 46-54.

PAGE 14
Over 10 minutes Multi-Girl creates 40 duplicates, but only the last four remain by the last of the 10 minutes.

PAGE 15
No. Optiman's speed is 40 m.p.h.

PAGE 16
Doc Zero's targets are forming a large zero.

The gaps to be filled are 1,6; 5,10; 8,9; and 10,5.

PAGE 17

$24 \div 8 - 3 = 0$
$2 \times 6 \div 3 - 4 = 0$
$3 \times 7 \div 3 - 7 = 0$
(Numbers 3, 3, and 7)

PAGE 18

Divide the miles per hour by 60 to make miles per minute. The Infini-car travels at 2 miles/min, so it will take 3 mins to travel 6 miles. The Infini-cycle travels at $1\frac{1}{2}$ miles/min. It will take 2 mins for 3 miles. The Infini-copter travels at 4 miles/min. It will take 1 min for 4 miles. The bus travels at 1 mile/min. It will take 2 mins for 2 miles. So the Infini-copter would arrive first.

PAGE 19

The windows are smashed in the order 2, 3, 5, 7, 11, 13, 17: prime numbers!
The next two numbers would be 19 and 23.

PAGE 20

From left to right: $\frac{3}{4}$, $\frac{2}{3}$, $\frac{1}{2}$, $\frac{1}{3}$, $\frac{1}{4}$.

PAGE 21

The blasters are firing from odd, then even-numbered cannons going up, then odd and even-numbered cannons going down. So the next three beams will come from cannons 6, 4, and 2.

PAGE 22

Attack plan
A scores 44,
B scores 48,
C scores 46,
D scores 50,
... so only D could stop Optiman.

PAGE 23

The blocks on the left total 119. The blocks needed to prop up the building are 19, 25, 32, and 43.

PAGE 24

There are 35 people and 18 pets, so 13 Multi-Girls are needed.

PAGE 25

Doc Zero has 4 Magno Mines, 8 Stun Strikes, plus 24 Scare Flares to begin with. He fires 3 Magno Mines, 9 Scare Flares, and 5 Stun Strikes, so he is left with 1 Magno Mine, 3 Stun Strikes, and 15 Scare Flares.

PAGE 26

Going clockwise from the triangle, the shapes have an increasing number of sides, except for the square between the octagon and hexagon.

PAGE 27

$5 \times 3 + 4 = 19$
$7 \times 2 + 11 = 25$
$9 \times 3 - 6 = 21$
$30 \div 6 + 12 = 17$
$4 \times 6 \div 3 = 8$
$33 \div 11 + 12 = 15$.
The missing symbols
are +, x, -, +, ÷, +.

PAGE 28

Divide the total
$(50\% + 50\% + 30\%$
$+ 30\%)$ by the number
of engines (4).
$160\% \div 4 = 40\%$.

PAGE 29

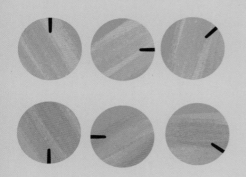

PAGE 30

20 seconds.

PAGE 31

$41 - 19 - 22 = 0$,
$38 - 23 - 15 = 0$,
$34 - 14 - 20 = 0$,
$27 - 17 - 10 = 0$,
$25 - 12 - 13 = 0$.

PAGE 32

The numbers form the
infinity symbol.

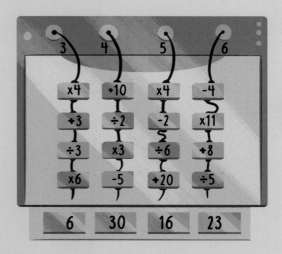

CHAPTER 2

PAGE 35

Wire $3 \times 4 + 3 \div 3 \times 6 = 30$
Wire $4 + 10 \div 2 \times 3 - 5 = 16$
Wire $5 \times 4 - 2 \div 6 + 20 = 23$
Wire $6 - 4 \times 11 + 8 \div 5 = 6$

PAGE 36

$4^2 = 16$, $5^2 = 25$, $6^2 = 36$, $7^2 = 49$,
$8^2 = 64$, $9^2 = 81$.

PAGE 37

The blue gem on the left is the
only one without a line
of symmetry.

PAGE 38

$0.1 = \frac{1}{10}$, $0.25 = \frac{1}{4}$, $0.5 = \frac{1}{2}$,
$0.6 = \frac{3}{5}$, $0.7 = \frac{7}{10}$, $1.25 = \frac{5}{4}$,
$1.5 = \frac{3}{2}$, $1.75 = \frac{7}{4}$.

PAGE 39

A = 4, B= 6, C= 9.

PAGE 40

The blue and yellow gems that
are next to each other have the
same number of sides, decreasing;
the pink one's number of sides is
decreasing as well. So the next
two would be a blue triangle and
a yellow triangle.

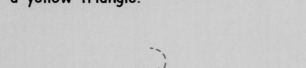

PAGE 41

		210			
		99	111		
	47	52	59		
	24	23	29	30	
14	10	13	16	14	
10	4	6	7	9	5

PAGE 42

The highest prime number is 23.

PAGE 43

The dragon's riddle: 13
32 is not a square number.

PAGE 44

XI for 11.

PAGE 45

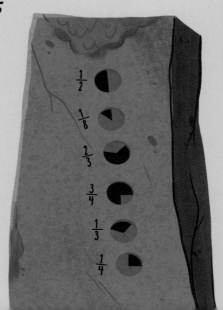

$\frac{1}{2}$

$\frac{1}{8}$

$\frac{2}{3}$

$\frac{3}{4}$

$\frac{1}{3}$

$\frac{1}{4}$

PAGE 46

12 can be exactly divided by
6, 14 by 7, 15 by 5, 27 by 9,
32 by 8, 33 by 11.

PAGE 47

The white route adds up
to the highest number: 25.

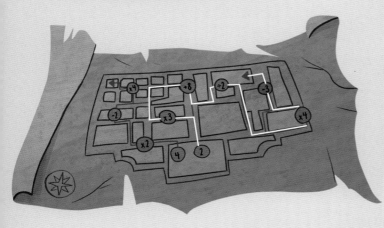

PAGE 48

PAGE 49

$\frac{1}{4}$	30
0.5	6^2
$5\frac{1}{4}$	8^2
5.4	$80\frac{1}{2}$
15	80.75
4^2	

PAGE 50

48

PAGE 51

10

PAGE 52

The scarab gem is numbered
48 (3 x 16).

PAGE 53

44 ÷ 11 = 4
48 ÷ 8 = 6
35 ÷ 7 = 5
27 ÷ 3 = 9
42 ÷ 6 = 7
36 ÷ 12 = 3

PAGE 54

The correct gem is marked
with a white cross.

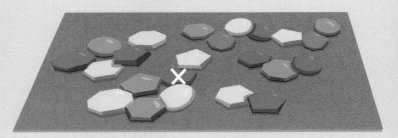

PAGE 55

30% of the gems are blue, 25% are pink, and 40% are oval.

PAGE 56

Pink gems: 50% or $\frac{1}{2}$.

Blue gems 25% or $\frac{1}{4}$,

Yellow gems: 25% or $\frac{1}{4}$,

Other gems: 10% or $\frac{1}{10}$.

PAGE 57

I = 7, L = 22, M = 24, N = 12, O = 15, S = 4, and U = 18, so the magic word is SOLUMINOS!

PAGE 58

Each group needs 1 red, 1 blue, 2 pink, and 5 yellow.

PAGE 59

60 is exactly divisible by 1, 2, 3, 4, and 5.

PAGE 60

Cleo chooses wand number 9. 34 - 25 = 9.

CHAPTER 3

PAGE 63

A = 8, C= 2, E = 4, L = 1, T = 6. The message says "ASSEMBLE CREW AT LAUNCH CONTROL RIGHT AWAY"

PAGE 64

Earth worlds at 5:9 and 8:6 are in Calculon space.

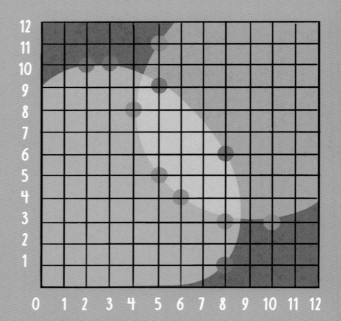

PAGE 65

32. One and one-third fuel rods are needed for every light year.

PAGE 66

The route resulting in the lowest number (11) is marked in white.

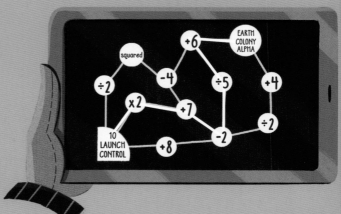

PAGE 67

$4^2 = 16$, $7^2 = 49$, $10^2 = 100$, $5^2 = 25$,
$3^2 = 9$, $8^2 = 64$, $12^2 = 144$,
$6^2 = 36$, $9^2 = 81$, $100^2 = 10000$.

PAGE 68

Route marked in white, below.

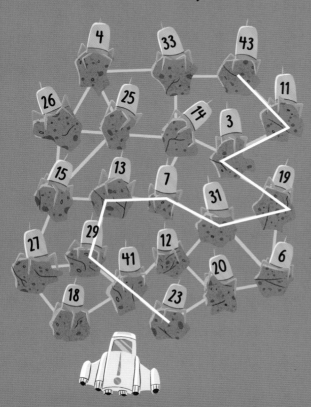

PAGE 69

No, it can't! 25% of 60 is 15, so the safe orbital range is 45–75.

PAGE 70

They're too soon! They should have waited 125 days.

PAGE 71

$10 \times 8 = 80$, $9 \times 4 = 36$, $5 \times 12 = 60$, $80 + 36 + 60 = 176$. $176 \div 4 = 44$.

PAGE 72

Route marked in white, below.

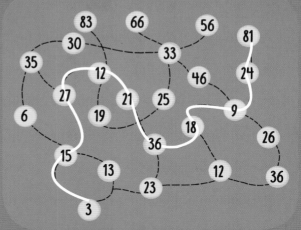

PAGE 73

The prime numbers are 2, 3, 5, 7, 11, 13, 17, 19, 23, and 29.

PAGE 74

There is no decimal matching $\frac{4}{5}$. The correct decimal would be 0.8 (not 0.9).

PAGE 75

$15 \div 3 - 5 = 0$
$4 \times 12 - 8 = 40$
$6 + 10 \div 2 = 8$
$40 - 15 \div 5 = 5$
$32 \div 4 - 6 = 2$
$9 \times 3 + 5 = 32$

PAGE 76

The answers are 5, 1, 18, 20, 8, so the planet is EARTH!

PAGE 77

The sequence adds 2, then 3, 4, etc, to the last number. 4 + 2= 6, 6 + 3 = 9, 9 + 4 = 13, 13 + 5 = 18, so the next 5 numbers are 24, 31, 39, 48, 58.

PAGE 78

The route in pink is the shortest - adding up to 40.

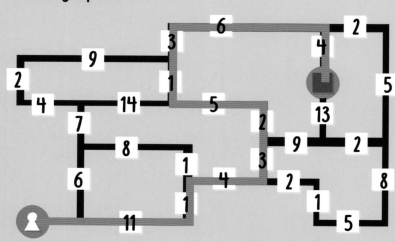

PAGE 79

9 x 7 = 63

29 - 17 = 12

25 + 9 + 5 = 39

21 ÷ 3 = 7

11 x 5 = 55

PAGE 80

3	X	6	-	11	=	7
X						X
6	X	2	÷	3	=	4
=				X		=
18		16	+	12	=	28
				=		
2	X	18	=	36		

PAGE 81

$\frac{1}{100}$ = 1% $\frac{1}{2}$ = 50%

$\frac{1}{25}$ = 4% $\frac{3}{5}$ = 60%

$\frac{1}{10}$ = 10% $\frac{3}{4}$ = 75%

$\frac{1}{5}$ = 20% $\frac{4}{5}$ = 80%

$\frac{1}{4}$ = 25% $\frac{3}{2}$ = 150%

PAGE 82

The correct answer is C.

A. The sequence adds 3, 5, 7, 9, so the next number is 36 (25 + 11).

B. The sequence adds 6 each time. 10, 16, 22, 28, 34, then 40, 46.

C. 84, 77, 70, 63, 56 is the 7 times table backward and continues with 49 and 42.

D. Adding the previous two numbers gives the next: 3, 5, 8, 13, 21, then 34, 55.

PAGE 83

Each engine's numbers should add up to 25.

Swap 1 and 8 on engines A and D, and swap 6 and 10 on engines B and C to make:

Engine A: 9, 8, 8
Engine B: 10, 10, 5
Engine C: 15, 6, 4
Engine D: 21, 3, 1

PAGE 84

Room A: 40,
Room B: 16,
Room C: 20,
Room D: 4.

PAGE 85

$5^2 + 12^2 = x^2$
$x^2 = 169$, so x = 13

PAGE 86

10 x 15 x 10 = 1,500

PAGE 87

3 x 5 x 2 = 30
7 x 2 + 6 = 20
100 ÷ 5 - 8 = 12
14 x 2 + 34 = 62
8 x 6 - 25 = 23
13 + 20 - 20 = 13

PAGE 88

	ESS PYTHAGORAS	PERCENTAGE INCREASE	ESS FIBONACCI
Speed	12	25%	15
Power	40	20%	48
Mass	2,000	10%	2,200
Length	300	5%	315
Crew quarters	8	75%	14

CHAPTER 4

PAGE 91

Dale and Daisy wind the hands of the pocket watch to...
12:10,
then 8:40,
then 10:05,
and finally 10:45.

PAGE 92

El Numero should be at coordinates 5,10.

PAGE 93

They sell the items worth $120, $270, $310, and $400.

PAGE 94

The flight from Townton to Miami arrives at 2:30pm (Townton time.) The flight from Miami to Star City leaves at 3:30pm and arrives at 8pm (Townton time.) The flight from Star City to Santa Luna leaves at 9pm and arrives at 11pm (Townton time, again.) Because Santa Luna is 8 hours ahead, it is now 7am local time.

PAGE 95

No. The boats have digits that add up to 38, 36, 39, and 35.

PAGE 96

No, the captain would beat his father's record in 12 years, not ten. He is not who he claims to be.

PAGE 97

46%

PAGE 98

The boat sails 12 squares north, 6 east, 2 south, 8 east, 4 north and 2 west.

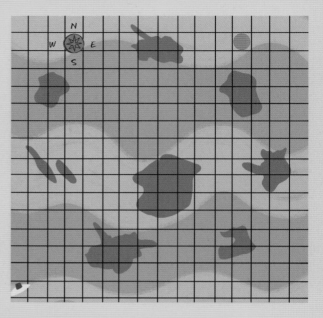

PAGE 99

60 x 4 ÷ 10 = 24 buckets of water.

PAGE 100

PAGE 101
25%

PAGE 102
Each number has one more added to it than the last. Numbers next in the sequence are: 16, 22, 29, 37.

PAGE 103
15 steps ahead, 1 step to the right.

PAGE 104
From lowest to highest, the order is 0.25, 1/3, 0.5, 1.2, 5/4, 2.2, 2^2, 4.5.

PAGE 105
The route follows the 9 times table, so the route is 9, 18, 27, 36, 45, 54, 63, 72, 81, 90, 99, 108.

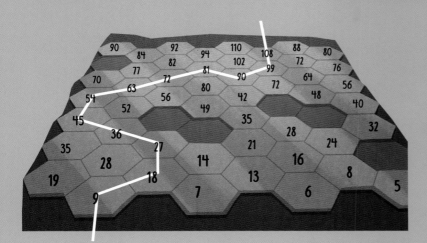

PAGE 106
Yes. It will take them 9.5 seconds to escape.

PAGE 107
The balance needs seven stones.

PAGE 108
13 x 5 - 2 = 63

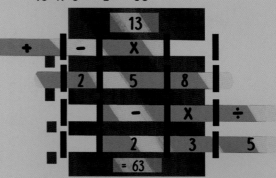

PAGE 109
1088. If 3761 is 2019, 2673 was 931.

PAGE 110

PAGE 111

2	9	4
7	5	3
6	1	8

PAGE 112

13.

PAGE 113

1,100.

PAGE 114

5 and 7.

PAGE 115

The group must remove
3, 15, 23, and 33. This leaves
8 + 11 + 31 = 50.

PAGE 116

The letters of the alphabet have
been replaced by numbers
in order from 1 to 26, so
6, 1, 13, 9, 12, 25 = FAMILY.

This book belongs to:

....